Inventions That Shaped the World

The Automobile

R O B Y N   C O N L E Y

Franklin Watts
A Division of Scholastic Inc.
New York • Toronto • London • Auckland • Sydney
Mexico City • New Delhi • Hong Kong
Danbury, Connecticut

Dedication

Thanks to Mr. O for his expertise and patience

Photographs © 2005: Bob Italiano: cover top right, 46; Brown Brothers: chapter openers, 12, 16, 17 inset, 19, 20, 24, 27 bottom, 31, 32, 34 top, 36, 38, 43, 56, 18; campbellriversales.com: cover center left; Corbis Images: cover bottom left, 34 bottom, 51, 59 (Bettmann), 10 (Tom Grill/Royalty-Free), 21 (E.O. Hoppé), cover top left (Lester Lefkowitz), 50 (Danny Lehman), 9 (Louis K. Meisel Gallery, Inc.), 52 (Charles O'Rear), 35 (Reuters), 48 (Paul A. Souders), 6 (Tom Stewart), 67 (Tom Wagner), 61 (Nik Wheeler), cover bottom right (Peter Yates); Culver Pictures: 13, 25; David R. Frazier: 53; General Motors Corporation: cover center right; Getty Images: 42 (Greg Ceo), 57 (Jonathan Ferrey), 22 (MPI); Hulton|Archive/Getty Images: 28, 29, 27 top; From the Collections of The Henry Ford: 40; Masterfile/Segel & Kranefeld/Zefa: 45; North Wind Picture Archives: 11, 17; PhotoEdit: 69 (Myrleen Ferguson Cate), 7 (A. Ramey), 62 (Mark Richards), 66 (David Young-Wolff); WireImage.com/Toxteth O'Grady/LAT USA: 58.

Cover design by Robert O'Brien
Book production by Tricia Griffiths Swatko

Library of Congress Cataloging-in-Publication Data

Conley, Robyn.
    The automobile / Robyn Conley.—1st ed.
        p. cm. — (Inventions that shaped the world)
    Includes bibliographical references and index.
    ISBN 0-531-12333-2 (lib. bdg.)   0-531-16719-4 (pbk.)
    1. Automobiles—History—Juvenile literature. 2. Popular culture—Juvenile literature. I. Title. II. Series.

    TL147.C567 2005
    629.222—dc22   2004006825

Contents

Behind the Wheel

Dozens of automakers have come and gone during the past one hundred years. Some of their names are still familiar today. We hear "Ford" and "Chrysler" in television ads and see them on car-dealership signs. Maybe you have a favorite make of automobile.

Traveling to school would be tough without some form of automobile. Yellow buses deliver students to their homes and schools, sporting events, and field trips. Huge semitrailer trucks, sometimes called tractor-trailer rigs or semis for short, deliver milk and food to school lunchrooms. Smaller vans haul packages of books to your library and mail to your principal. Your teacher might drive a pickup, a sedan, or an economy car.

Look all around your town or city. Many of its basic functions depend on vehicles. People who work in fire departments, police stations, and hospitals would have

Transportation plays a daily role in most lives. School buses transport students to and from school every day.

trouble doing their jobs without the right type of automobile to help them. Without a vehicle, how would all of the community's trash move from garbage cans to the landfills? How would the electric companies fix the electric lines high in the sky without those big bucket trucks to raise the technicians into the sky?

The invention of motorized vehicles changed American culture in a number of ways. The invention led to the expansion of the many related industries that had to do with

The face of transportation has changed worldwide, with businesses and families depending on motorized travel.

the making of the automobile. This expansion created new jobs, and the creation of new jobs led to the need for more managers. Managers helped keep workers content in their jobs and aided in creating smooth-running operations throughout the automotive industry.

Even so, as the companies that contributed to the manufacture of motorized vehicles grew larger, and more employees were needed, problems sometimes arose between management and the workers. Workers in other industries had formed unions that elected officers to talk to management to negotiate wages and working conditions. Soon the automotive industry developed unions as well.

Soon, roads were constructed that crisscrossed the nation. This allowed motorized vehicles to travel to more places, and create a major change in culture. The automobile offered its purchasers the ability to travel great distances with more ease. Relatives who wanted to meet family members who lived far away—and with whom they may have only kept in touch by letter writing—could now load up their cars and hit the open road.

Before long, businesses that appealed to travelers popped up on the sides of roadways. Some of these included motels and diners that offered clean rooms and decent meals at reasonable prices. Naturally, gas stations also became abundant in every town across the country.

With the advent of motorized travel, new businesses sprang up, such as roadside diners for hungry travelers.

Over time the railroads that had served to transport people throughout the states were used less often. Families and individuals enjoyed taking to the road in their own vehicles to explore whatever adventure the trip might bring.

Motorized travel is essential to the functioning of today's cities and businesses. Would you believe that all these modern vehicles were based on a simple design similar to that of a tricycle? Because of that initial design, the first

Automobiles have given families the freedom to explore new places.

motorized car came into production. It forever changed the
world of transportation, moving consumers of cities around
the globe out of the horse and cart and into an automobile.

The Road to Change

Statistics show us that in 1900, most people never traveled more than a total of 1,200 miles (2,000 kilometers) during their entire lives. This is because they did most of that traveling on foot or on horseback. Walking everywhere or riding on horseback kept many people from visiting towns or states too far from home. It also limited

Before motor vehicles were available, people traveled from one place to another by foot.

how much of a farmer's crop could be carried into town to trade. This lack of efficient transportation made some people long for faster ways to travel. At the turn of the century, the few people who could afford to purchase automobiles started taking more and more rides into the rural countryside. Now people who had only ridden in horse-drawn wagons could see firsthand these newfangled machines.

Before today's modern automobile emerged, wagons and carriages pulled by horses were the main forms of transportation. There were some attempts made at propelling a wagon. In the late 1700s a few steam-powered vehicles were built. In 1769 the French engineer Nicholas Cugnot tried several different designs with some success.

During the late 1800s, horse-drawn wagons and carriages were used to carry goods and people from place to place.

There were even a few recorded races featuring the cumbersome machines he built. The main problem with steam engines, however, was their heavy weight and large size. This factor made steam engines difficult to use in smaller vehicles, but steam-powered locomotives used to perform farmwork and to move large loads worked very well. The invention of huge steam locomotives also led to the passage of the first traffic law.

In 1865 the British government passed the Locomotives on Highways Act (Red Flag Act). This act regulated the way

In the late 1700s steam-powered vehicles were invented, but their size and weight made them difficult to navigate.

heavy-traction engines moved on common roadways. The vehicles were limited to speeds of 4 miles (6.4 km) per hour in the country, and 2 miles (3.2 km) per hour in the city. This act also required three men to travel with each locomotive. One had to steer; one had to stoke, or feed, the engine; and one had to walk 15 feet (4.5 meters) ahead of the vehicle at all times. The man out front waved a red flag if the driver needed to be warned about a road condition or another driver coming in his direction.

A few years later horse-drawn carriages were still the main mode of transportation. Horses pulled carriages that had wooden wheels and boxy frames. By 1885, however, these horse-drawn carriages began sharing roads with gasoline-powered carriages.

More Growth and a New Name

The greatest changes that came about just after gas-powered vehicles became popular involved industry growth and the creation of new jobs relating to the automotive industry. Another important change dealt with the naming of these machines. Most people referred to them as "horseless carriages." After all, most of the original designs contained a carriage and a motor. The term made sense, but lacked style. A change came in 1899 when the *New York Times* referred to them as "automobiles."

IT'S ALL IN A NAME

In 1899, after the *New York Times* used the term "automobile," many readers wrote letters to the paper, which the editors printed. A debate followed about the word *automobile* and its true meaning. Someone wrote in saying that it might be a word that was half Greek and half Latin in origin. After this letter appeared the paper was swamped with replies. Each reader wanted to rename the machine and insisted that his or her idea was the best. Some suggestions from across the United States were goalone, petrocar, motocycle, and *quadracycle*.

Perhaps the name "automobile" stuck, because in September 1899 a new magazine titled *The Automobile* was published. This publication featured many articles about automobiles and defended the use of the term. One thing was certain: Americans had embraced the new machine and its name with gusto.

New Jobs Are Created

All the advances in motorized travel helped other major industries emerge in the 1900s. Motorized vehicles could speed the delivery of goods to their destinations without the operators having to feed and care for horses. There were problems, however, such as mending broken wheels or

Problems with dependability and reliability were common in the automobile's early years. However, as the industry grew, technology progressed and problems occurred less often.

performing engine adjustments that sometimes caused delays. Motorists during this time period had to know more than just driving techniques. They also had to be their own mechanics. Yet when motorized vehicles became more reliable, their benefits became unquestionable.

HARVEY FIRESTONE'S BETTER TIRES

One thing that helped the automobile's future was the invention of a better tire by Harvey Firestone (below). Born in 1868 in Columbiana County, Ohio, Firestone became one of the most respected tire makers in the world. In 1890, after working at a buggy manufacturing company, Firestone opened his own business making rubber tires for carriages. By 1896 he was making tires for automobiles. He began working with Henry Ford in 1904.

As the years passed, Firestone's company introduced new and more reliable types of tires, such as those with nonskid treads, pneumatic (air-filled) tires, and low-pressure balloon tires, as well as farm tractor tires. By the time of his death in 1938, Firestone's Firestone Tire & Rubber Company had earned a strong reputation in the automobile industry.

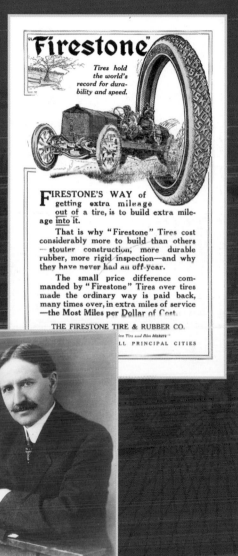

"Firestone"

Tires hold the world's record for durability and speed.

FIRESTONE'S WAY of getting extra mileage out of a tire, is to build extra mileage into it.

That is why "Firestone" Tires cost considerably more to build than others — stouter construction, more durable rubber, more rigid inspection—and why they have never had an off-year.

The small price difference commanded by "Firestone" Tires over tires made the ordinary way is paid back, many times over, in extra miles of service —the Most Miles per Dollar of Cost.

THE FIRESTONE TIRE & RUBBER CO.

ALL PRINCIPAL CITIES

The use of more reliable motorized vehicles in cities helped police departments, fire departments, and hospitals. As automobile makers learned better and faster ways to produce cars, cars became less expensive. More and more people started buying and driving these four-wheeled, gas-powered vehicles. Because of this increase in demand, more and more jobs were created. Some jobs had to do with keeping roads in good condition. More police officers were needed to keep traffic problems under control in cities where

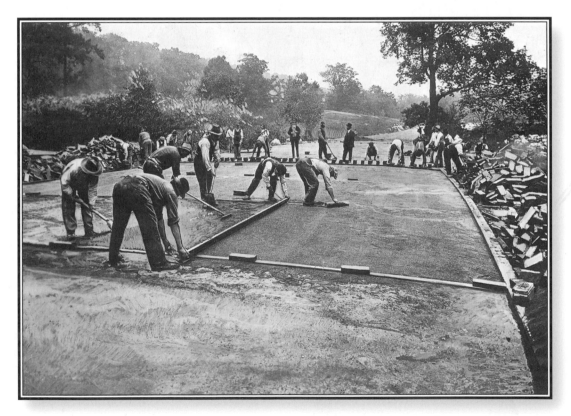

The automobile industry created jobs for other industries such as upholstering, sales, and road construction (above).

busy intersections could cause major accidents. Some jobs not as obvious as traffic control also experienced direct growth due to the production of increasing numbers of automobiles. For example, all of the glass needed for windshields and windows boosted jobs and sales in the glass industry. All of the rubber needed for tires created jobs and sales in the rubber industry. All of the leather needed to upholster seats created jobs and sales in the leather industry. And all of the paint required to cover the exteriors of the automobiles created jobs and sales in the paint industry.

Jobs also popped up for mechanics to repair the vehicles and for salespeople to sell the vehicles. The cars had to be moved from the factory by train or other means, which also

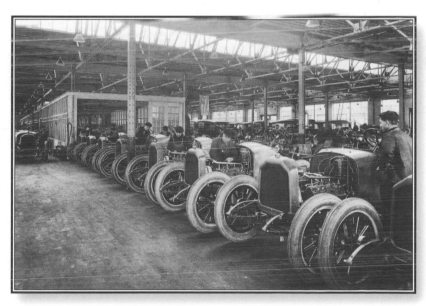

The production of automobiles produced many jobs, creating a huge amount of industrial growth for automobile manufacturers.

supplied jobs to those who transported the cars. Banks financed automobile loans, which brought new customers to the banks.

Recreation and Sport

Another job related to automobile production was that of the specialty designers who created kits that could turn a vehicle into a tent or a camper. These designers invented the first recreational vehicles (RVs). Some historians argue that the

Some automobile designers combined recreation and transportation. By converting an automobile to a camper, people had an affordable way to travel and to vacation.

original American RV was the Conestoga wagon that many families traveled and lived in while settling the West. Actually, the first RVs pulled by motorized vehicles were based on the Conestoga wagon's design.

TELESCOPES AND TINNIES

A "telescope" style wagon, dating back to 1916, received its name because of the way it folded up in sections like a telescope folds up into itself. These types of camping vehicles unfolded into cooking areas and living areas. Some even came with collapsible tents.

By 1936 more than ten thousand camping trailers had been built, and more than fifteen thousand campgrounds had been established in the United States (above). Camping was an affordable way for young families to travel across the country and visit new places. Many city residents didn't like these traveling families who parked their tents and campers in empty lots or in neighborhood parks. These campers were sometimes called "tinnies." The name came from the tin cans that these families often used to hold their food. Canned foods were easy to pack and use on the road.

Henry Ford (left), Thomas Edison (second from left), and Harvey Firestone (fifth from left) pictured with friends, on a camping trip in July 1921

Some of the most famous campers were three friends who were very involved with the automobile: Henry Ford, Harvey Firestone, and Thomas Edison. Many photographs exist of the three cooking and chatting around their campfires, proving that even the most hardworking men enjoyed a chance to travel in these marvelous recreational vehicles.

Auto Racing

Another exciting activity created because of the invention of the automobile was the sport of auto racing. The earliest races took place in Europe, where the automobile had its start. In 1898 Fernand Charron was the first man to win a race that crossed international borders. The drivers started in Paris, France, went to Amsterdam in the Netherlands, and then back to Paris. The top speed was about 27 miles (43 km) per hour.

A few years later in the United States, one of the most famous original racing cars was the Thomas Flyer. It became popular while involved in a race around the world that began in New York City and ended in Paris. Referred to as The Great Race, this race began on February 12, 1908, in Times Square with nearly 250,000 people watching the start. Over the next 170 days, the drivers and their crews—usually two other team members who helped drive and maintain the automobile—covered 12,427 land miles (20,000 km, and more than 22,000 miles overall, including sea voyages). The man driving the Thomas Flyer was George Schuster. He was the only crew member to travel the entire distance. He drove the car into Paris to win the race. There has not been another attempt at a round-the-world auto race since 1908. Therefore, the Thomas Flyer still holds the world's record for speed.

George Schuster and his crew in the famous Thomas Flyer during "The Great Race"

Races of all types grew in size and popularity as the years passed. This new sport helped create jobs for drivers, pit crews, racing-event organizers, and racing-car manufacturers.

Without a doubt, the automobile helped change the way Americans and the world traveled, worked, and played. The people who invented and built the first automobiles were responsible for making this possible.

CHAPTER THREE

The Men Who Started the World Driving

Many Americans might think Henry Ford invented the first automobile. He did build a popular type of car, but before Henry Ford's famous Model T could be built, a few other inventions had to be perfected. The most important invention was the **four-stroke**, **gas-powered engine** perfected by Nikolaus Otto in 1876.

Otto was a German engineer whose gas-powered engine changed the way automobiles were powered. He based his

Nikolaus Otto's design for an effective gas motor was one of the most important contributions to engine design.

designs on a **two-stroke engine** that was invented by Jean Lenoir in 1859. The problem with Lenoir's two-stroke engine was that it overheated easily. Also, the **ignition system** used to create an electric current to start the motor was unreliable. It worked for small machines, such as printing presses. Nikolaus Otto improved on the basic design and created a stronger motor.

TWO-STROKE AND FOUR-STROKE ENGINES

A two-stroke engine only uses two steps to create heat. This engine has limits because it uses a fuel and oil mixture that runs continuously through the *piston chamber*. This makes the engine run hot, which causes parts to wear out after only short time periods, so repairs are often needed.

A four-stroke engine uses four steps to create heat. It uses a fuel and air mix, which runs cleaner than the two-stroke engine and creates more power.

Karl Benz

A German mechanical engineer, Karl Benz, was instrumental in early automobile engineering. In 1886 Benz had constructed a gasoline-powered engine mounted into a tricycle body. It had three wire wheels and a water-cooled, four-stroke engine. The engine had only 1 horsepower, but it was strong enough to carry a couple of passengers. On

January 29, 1886, Karl Benz was issued a patent for his "carriage with gas engine."

Karl Friedrich Benz was born in Germany in 1844. His father died when Karl was only two years old, but his mother worked hard to provide for her son. After they settled in Karlsruhe, Germany, Benz received a technical education and became an engineer.

German engineer and car manufacturer Karl Benz

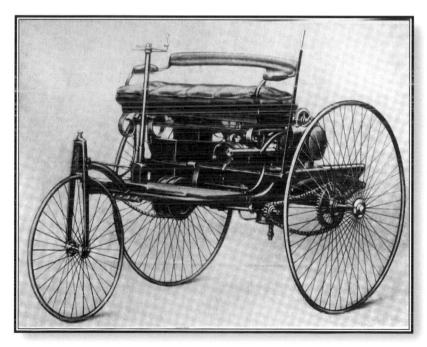

Karl Benz designed his three-wheeled vehicle as a means to overcome steering problems. However, roads at that time were not favorable for a three-wheeled design.

He worked for several companies before forming his own business. Over the next ten years Benz and his partner, August Ritter, worked to develop a new design for a two-stroke engine, which later was adapted into a four-stroke system.

Benz first used his engines to supply power to many items other than motorized vehicles. His interest in vehicles grew, however, and his company even participated in some of the first automobile races.

One thing Benz had trouble with was managing his business. His company faced several rough periods, and by the time Benz reached eighty years old, he had to merge his company with one owned by engineer Gottlieb Daimler, a fellow German, to survive in the automotive industry.

Gottlieb Daimler

Also instrumental in the history of the automobile was Gottlieb Daimler. He and his partner, Wilhelm Maybach, worked in Otto's factory. Later, after leaving the company, they created a lightweight, faster, four-stroke, gas-powered

Gottlieb Daimler (above) and his design partner, Wilhelm Maybach, improved upon Otto's engine by designing an engine very similar to today's gas engine.

engine. At this time the fastest four-stroke engine achieved only 130 revolutions per minute (rpm). Daimler and Maybach's design reached 900 rpm. In 1889 they installed their engine onto a carriage and became the first men to build a gas-powered, four-wheeled vehicle.

Daimler and Maybach's first four-wheeled vehicle

THE DAIMLER MOTOR COMPANY

Gottlieb Daimler wanted to expand the uses for his unique engine. He talked with William Steinway, who was the owner of Steinway and Sons piano manufacturers. Steinway already had a factory in Hartford, Connecticut, and Daimler hoped to sell his cars in the United States. He believed that Steinway could give him the space needed to build cars in America.

In 1890, under the ownership of Steinway, Daimler Motor Company was founded and over time became respected for its quality automobiles. Its cars were fast and reliable. Their design consisted of a four-speed *transmission*. A transmission consists of gears in various sizes. Smaller gears allow the car to go faster, similar to gears on a bicycle. Adding smaller gears helped Daimler's cars reach speeds of up to 10 miles (16 km) per hour.

By 1891 the Daimler Motor Company had designed engines to be used in tramway cars, carriages, quadracycles, fire engines, and even some boats.

The automobile industry might have started in Europe, but Americans caught up and surpassed the productivity of the Europeans in no time.

American Inventors

In the early 1890s two American brothers started building their first gasoline-powered, wheeled vehicle. Charles and Frank Duryea used their bicycle-building skills to help them build their first car, which they designed in 1893. Three years later, in 1896, the Duryea Motor Wagon Company had sold thirteen models of its Duryea vehicle, making the brothers the first American manufacturer to sell so many cars in one year.

Another early American automaker was Ransom Eli Olds. His company, the Olds Motor Vehicle Company of Detroit, was founded in 1899. The company first tried building luxury vehicles but did not have much success selling them. When the company came out with a unique curved dash

The popularity of the Olds curved dash design increased sales for the manufacturer.

design in 1901, it sold six hundred of that model for $650 each. By 1904 Olds was selling up to five thousand of his curved dash cars. This level of production marked Olds as the first automobile manufacturer to mass-produce cars in the United States.

Henry Ford

Perhaps the most recognized early automobile maker in the United States was Henry Ford. His career began on a farm located only a few miles from the city that would become known around the world for its automobiles.

Henry Ford was born July 30, 1863, to William and Mary Ford in an area now called Dearborn, Michigan. Henry was the oldest of six children. He attended a one-room school and helped with farm chores during his childhood. A special quality of Henry's was his ability to fix mechanical things at an early age.

When Ford turned sixteen, he left the farm to work in Detroit as an apprentice, which

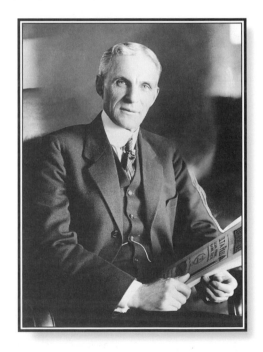

Henry Ford wanted to produce a vehicle that was well priced, dependable, and efficient.

is a person learning a skill or trade. Ford was an apprentice machinist, so he learned how to build and repair all types of machines, especially steam engines. For the next three years Ford learned his new trade while sometimes returning to the farm to help with the crops or to repair the family's farm equipment.

In 1888 Ford married a young woman named Clara Bryant. He also took on the new position of running a sawmill. His true desire, though, was to work on his own mechanical ideas. This was fulfilled when he started working as an engineer for the Edison Illuminating Company in 1891. Thomas Edison's company brought electricity and lighting to American homes.

By 1893 Ford was promoted to chief engineer in Edison's company. This earned him the extra money he needed to work on his designs for better internal combustion engines. In June of 1896, his experiments succeeded when Ford completed his own self-propelled vehicle, the quadracyle.

Ford's quadracyle had four wire wheels similar to extra-sturdy bicycle wheels. He steered it with a tiller, like the kind used on a boat, rather than with a steering wheel. After working out many business and production details, he finally had a machine he believed he could produce at a profit. He founded the Ford Motor Company in 1903. Ford served as vice-president and chief engineer of his company and soon began producing the Model A.

Henry Ford and his first vehicle, the quadracycle

In 1903, Ford opened this two-story building in Detroit, Michigan. In less than two years, production was so great that he had to open a larger plant in the same city.

The Model A sold for $850. It had an 8-horse-power engine, which meant it had the same strength as eight horses. The engine was located under the driver's seat. A handle had to be cranked to get the engine started. Ford replaced the steering tiller with a steering wheel on the Model A, but the wheels were made of wooden spokes, unlike those of the quadracycle. The Model A could reach a speed of almost 30 miles (48 km) per hour, and it became a popular car. From

A 1903 Model A at the Ford World Headquarters in Dearborn, Michigan

June of 1903 until March of 1904, Ford sold 658 of these cars.

In its early years the Ford Motor Company produced fewer than ten cars a day. Workers in groups of two or three would build one car at a time from the ground up with parts made by other companies. Two things inspired Ford to do away with this system. First, he wanted to produce more cars in a shorter time in his factory. Second, he wanted to build cars that were more reliable, efficient, and reasonably priced than the Model A. This dream created a revolution in manufacturing and made Ford famous.

The Model T and the Assembly Line

When Ford realized the need for a lower-priced car that was easy to repair, he worked to design a car he called the Model T. Introduced in 1908, the Model T decreased Ford's production costs from $850 a day in 1906 to $400 a day by 1916, and to only $290 a day by 1924. Ford's insightful cost-cutting innovations—especially the automobile assembly-line production method he instituted that was based on other industries' processes—finally made cars affordable for more people in the United States.

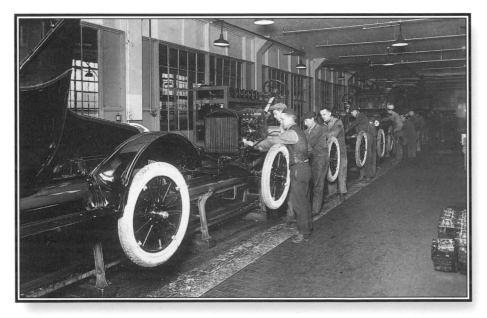

Ford's assembly line cut costs, making cars more affordable. This photo shows Ford's Model Ts on the assembly line.

FORD'S COST-CUTTING IDEAS

The Model T became affordable for so many people because Henry Ford figured out a way to make more cars at a faster rate for less money. One reason his production costs were reduced was that Ford started manufacturing his own parts that were faster to assemble and cheaper to use. Another reason is that he began painting every car black, because that color paint dried the fastest.

His most important innovation was changing how a car moved through the factory. Instead of one group of workers building one car from the ground up, Ford gave each group of workers a specialized task, such as installing the tires. Then the car moved to another group that installed another part.

Because of Ford's success with the Model T and the assembly-line system, he was considered a pioneer and a genius in the automobile industry.

Patent Troubles

Ford had his share of trouble, however, because he refused to pay royalties to a man named George Selden. In 1895 Selden, an attorney from Rochester, New York, was granted a patent for a self-propelled vehicle that was powered by a four-stroke, internal-combustion engine. He called it a "road engine."

Although Selden wasn't the only inventor of a vehicle powered by an internal-combustion four-stroke engine, he

George Selden and his "road engine." A patent for his four-stroke engine required all automakers to pay him a royalty, which Ford refused to do.

did earn the patent. Because he had a patent, he wanted all auto manufacturers to pay him a royalty, which was a small percentage of their profits, if they used an engine design similar to his.

Most automakers who used a similar engine chose to pay a percentage of their profits to Selden rather than fight his patent claim in court. They formed an alliance called the Association of Licensed Automobile Manufacturers (ALAM).

Companies that joined this alliance paid Selden royalties to avoid lawsuits that he might bring against them for building cars.

Because Ford refused to join ALAM, Selden brought a lawsuit against him in October 1903. The lawsuit was battled in the courts for eight years until Ford Motor Company won the case in 1911. This victory turned Ford into a folk hero across the nation.

Ford's Other Interests

Henry Ford's success and notoriety encouraged him to speak out about his opinions on political issues. He didn't care if he offended people with his statements. One example of Ford being outspoken was when President Woodrow Wilson called out the National Guard to help stop Pancho Villa's raids along the Mexican border. Ford told his employees that they would lose their jobs if they answered the president's call. This attitude caused him to be scorned by some groups of people.

Ford was one of the first employers to offer decent wages to his employees to encourage them to remain with the company. He also paid each worker in cash so they wouldn't be tempted to spend part of their money in local taverns, which was where many people cashed their paychecks.

Some workers, however, didn't like the conditions that came with the higher wages. They were expected to work their shift without breaks if they couldn't make their quotas. Any worker who was an immigrant and had trouble speaking English had to take language courses offered by the company at night. Also, in order to receive the much-advertised $5.00 a day wage—a good wage at this time—employees first had to work for Ford for six months at a lower rate.

His business continued to grow, and Ford built an even bigger car plant in Dearborn, Michigan. It was completed in 1927. When he turned the company over to his son, Edsel, Ford Motor Company had earned a place in history as a major automaker.

Ford's English school was required by all employees who did not speak English.

How an Automobile Works

If you've ever looked under the hood of a car or truck, you've probably noticed lots of hoses, belts, and engine parts. Most cars differ in the way these parts are put together, but all modern-day cars' engines have the same purpose: to create power to propel the vehicle forward or backward, and to cool the engine so it doesn't overheat.

Ignition and Spark

It takes more than simply pumping gasoline into a gas tank to power an automobile. First the gas has to be ignited by a spark created by an electric current. This current is generated when a key is turned in the ignition switch and is completed when it reaches the **spark plug**. The **electric starter** receives its power from the vehicle's battery. Just like the batteries in video games and CD players, a car battery stores energy.

41

The first step in starting a car is ignition. A key turning in the ignition switch creates an electrical current that then ignites the gasoline.

EARLY IGNITION SYSTEMS

The first automobiles used magnetos to send an electric current to the spark plugs. *Magnetos* are small devices made up of magnets and coils of wire. Magnetos were activated when cranked by a hand crank in some of the first cars, similar to the way older airplanes were started by spinning the propeller to operate their magnetos. It

often took several cranks to activate the magneto in order for it to send enough electric current to the spark plugs. The main problem with magnetos was that they wore out easily. They also wore out their drivers with all that hand cranking! When the automotive engineers finally developed an electric starter, most motorists were quite happy to give up cranking their cars.

Powering and Propelling the Automobile

After the electric current reaches the spark plug, power is created by combustion. Combustion in today's car engine is an explosion that occurs when a mixture of air and fuel is ignited by the spark. The heat from this explosion is what powers the automobile.

When the compressed air-fuel mixture explodes, it puts the *crankshaft* into motion. This rotating motion turns gears that are located in the transmission, which controls the power coming from the crankshaft. On a rear-wheel-drive vehicle, the transmission gears turn the drive-shaft, which is a long, tubular connection to the rear axle. In the middle of that axle is a set of *differential* gears that turn the wheels. On a front-wheel-drive vehicle, the CV joints, which look like long arms reaching to the wheel, steer the vehicle. All these connected systems are what propel and turn the vehicle.

The transmission gears allow the car to move forward or backward. Most cars and trucks today have automatic transmissions that change gears with each increase or decrease in speed. Manual transmissions have gears that must be changed by the driver as the speed of the vehicle increases or decreases.

An important part of powering and propelling an automobile is the ability to stop it. The *brake system* engages when the brake pedal is pushed from inside the car. From there a line of pressure travels to the wheel, which creates friction at the wheels and slows the vehicle. Drum brakes apply friction by pushing outward on a drum-shaped device to which the wheel is bolted. Disc brakes apply friction by pinching both sides of a disc-shaped piece of metal to which the wheel is bolted. Both types of brakes are used on most vehicles today—discs in front, drums in back.

This driver is shifting gears manually. She must shift gears as the car speeds up and slows down.

Cooling the Automobile

All of this heat and combustion has to be cooled and regulated or the engine will run too hot and overheat. Most modern engines are kept at an optimum temperature by a

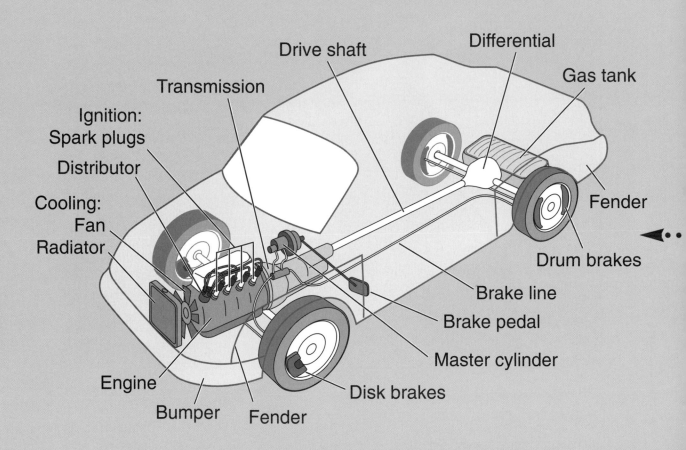

Drive shaft

Differential

Transmission

Gas tank

Ignition:
Spark plugs

Distributor

Cooling:
Fan
Radiator

Fender

Drum brakes

Brake line

Brake pedal

Master cylinder

Engine

Disk brakes

Bumper   Fender

water-cooling system in which water and a chemical called antifreeze are carried in hoses to the engine. Some engines are cooled with a fan that draws cool air through the radiator to cool the water before it returns to the engine block. Oil also helps to cool the vehicle when it flows between the engine's moving parts. It helps minimize friction so the parts won't get too hot or wear and scratch against each other.

Today's automobiles are comprised of several mechanical and electrical systems, which are connected to the vehicle's frame and body. Under the hood sit the engine, radiator, spark plugs, and other parts, as well as the ignition system's electrical wires and connections. The transmission, driveshaft, and differential are located beneath the body on the frame of the vehicle. All of these parts work together to move the vehicle forward and backward and faster and slower. They also enable the driver to steer the wheels in the direction he or she wants to go.

With these coordinating parts in the engine compartment and below the body, today's drivers can choose vehicles that are both mechanically strong and in a body style they prefer.

The Chassis

An automobile's frame is called a **chassis**. The first automobiles had frames built at local horse-carriage shops because the inventors chose to use designs already in use to support their motors. Over time, however, automakers chose to design their own frames for mounting the engines, wheels, and other parts.

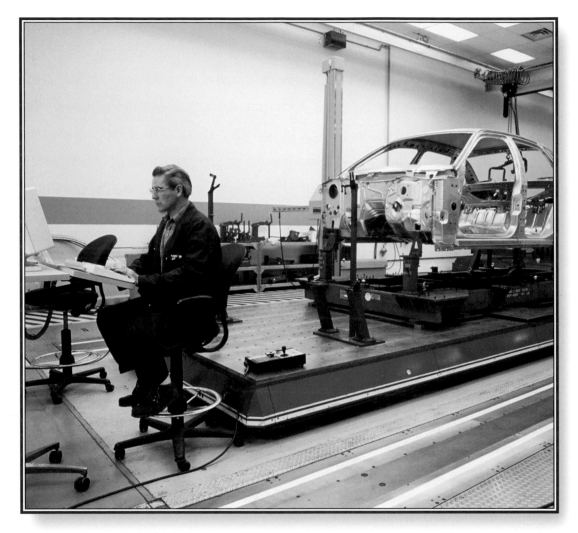

This chassis is being inspected at a Ford motor plant. A coordinate measuring machine creates a 3-D computer map to compare the chassis with its original specifications.

The basic chassis consists of the engine parts, the wheels and axles, and the body of the automobile. The body includes all the fenders, flooring, and sides, as well as the exterior lights and doors, steering wheel, and seats. These parts vary a great deal among automakers, which make some vehicles a better choice than others for each individual consumer.

Many design advances have improved automobile engines and body styles since their early years. Even so, the combustion of a compressed air-fuel mixture is what still powers today's vehicles.

Assembling the Automobile

Many of the products you buy today are put together by an assembly-line process. Some sandwich shops even use them when making your sandwich exactly as you want it. Assembly lines are systems that manufacturers use in which the product is sent throughout the factory on moving belts or tracks. As the product passes each station of workers, it receives a necessary part or process on its way to completion. In 1913 Henry Ford took the ideas that some meat-packaging companies used at the time to package meat and incorporated them in his auto manufacturing business.

The use of the assembly-line process made car manufacturing more efficient and therefore reduced production costs for auto manufacturers. Before long, all car companies followed Henry Ford's example of using the assembly line.

Assembly line workers at their station at a General Motors plant

THE STUDEBAKER ASSEMBLY LINE

When Studebaker cars were popular during the 1940s and 1950s, their South Bend, Indiana, plant had a two-floor assembly-line system. The frame and engine moved along in front of worker stations on the lower floor, while the upper body passed its workers on the upper floor. When the time came for  the body and engine to be joined, the upper body was lowered through an opening in the floor (above right). The final stages of manufacture were completed on the lower level.

One downside to the process, however, became obvious when a problem arose on the assembly line due to either a shortage of parts or a break in the conveyer belts. These disruptions could halt an entire work crew waiting down the line and back up the workers on the line before the break-down. Even so, as the assembly-line process was refined, these problems occurred less frequently and made the assembly line the most practical and cost-effective way to manufacture vehicles.

Today, assembly lines are often automated, with computerized robots attaching parts to cars and other products. The speed and accuracy of these machines have made human line workers obsolete in some industries. Human technicians, however, are still needed to maintain the machines and to program them, which makes the human touch every bit as essential to the assembly-line process today as it was in Henry Ford's original automobile plant.

Automated assembly lines are run by machines. In this photo, robots work on chassis.

A Driving Force Unleashed

There were only about eight thousand cars in the United States at the turn of the twentieth century, and nearly 500 million in the world at the turn of the twenty-first century. It is easy to see that the automobile has had a major impact since its early years. To comprehend this huge number of cars, imagine averaging the lengths of every small and medium-sized car, each city and

There are almost 500 million automobiles in the world!

tourist bus, every pickup, van, delivery truck, ambulance, and fire truck. You would get an average of 15 feet (4.6 m) per vehicle. Using that 15-foot figure, the 500 million automobiles lined up, bumper-to-bumper, would reach the moon and back three times. That's a lot of vehicles!

Farm Equipment

One area in which automobile technology helped everyday life profoundly was on the farm. Henry Ford became a key player in using his automobile engineering skills to aid farmers in their work. He remembered too well the pain and trouble that hard farmwork caused, and he wanted to ease these difficulties.

By 1907 Ford Motor Company had completed its first tractor. At the time it was called an "automobile plow." Henry Ford's dream was a success, and by 1910 farmers across the nation began using gas-powered tractors. Many farmers also converted Model Ts for use on their farms.

Popularity and Problems

The automobile continued to grow in popularity, and new car companies continued to form. Chevrolet began production in 1911, and in the 1920s General Motors (GM) began building luxury Cadillacs for the wealthy. Chevrolet also offered a car that was more stylish than the popular Model T and just as affordable.

As the next few decades passed, auto manufacturers made their buyers happy by making updates to the vehicles. Electric headlights lit up a driver's path. Windows that rolled up and down kept out heat and cold, wind and mud. People everywhere loved their cars and the independence automobiles gave them. One thing people did not like about this motorized travel, however, was the traffic it created.

More Traffic, More Roads

Too much traffic on small roadways created the need for better ways of managing traffic. For a time streets were shared by trolley cars, bicycles, horses, pedestrians, and cars. Accidents were common.

New police officers were trained to coordinate the flow of automobiles in cities. They stood in the middle of intersections and allowed each lane of traffic to move through one at a time. Later, electric traffic signals kept motorists driving and stopping when needed. The first three-colored traffic light was installed in Detroit, Michigan, in 1919. Engineers and electricians had to be trained to build and install these devices.

Better roads were also needed. Engineers had to plan new roadways and enlarge old ones to meet the demands put on the paths only carriages had once used. By 1956 a complete interstate highway system had been built across the United States to accommodate all the drivers.

This busy intersection was managed by a policeman who guided pedestrians and vehicles

Shutting Down for War

As the world faced two major wars in the first half of the twentieth century, the automobile manufacturers and their employees stopped making commercial vehicles. Some of the large automobile plants switched over to building war-related machinery and vehicles. Others shut down completely. The shortage of building materials and the lack of consumer interest in buying vehicles during financially difficult war times forced some smaller automakers out of business.

Another automobile-related industry that took a hit when wartime came was the racing industry. Most annual races were not held during World War I and World War II. When the wars were over, though, the races and their fans returned in a major way.

Massive Growth of the Racing Industry

Over the decades since the first auto race, racing of all types drew interest all across the country. There were races on straight tracks and round tracks, and even rallies that took place over a few days across various kinds of roads and obstacles.

Today, automobile racing is one of the most-watched sporting events in the world. Speedway tracks seat an average of 200,000 spectators. In comparison, football stadiums seat

In 2004, the Richmond International Raceway in Virginia hosted the NASCAR Nextel Cup Chevy American Revolution 400 to a packed house.

only an average of 50,000 to 80,000 fans. The National Association for Stock Car Auto Racing (NASCAR) sponsors many races each year. The publishers of *Media Sports Business*, reports, and newsletters estimate that by the year 2006, NASCAR will draw in nearly $3.4 billion per year.

THE INDY 500

One of the oldest and most popular racetracks in the United States is the Indianapolis 500 Motor Speedway in Indiana. The Indy 500 was built in 1909 and paved with 3.2 million bricks. Over the years the bricks have been paved over with asphalt for a smoother  driving surface, but a section of bricks is still visible at the start/finish line.

The race's name comes from the 500 miles driven during the race, all in a 2.5-mile circle, and all in one day. The first race took place in 1911 and awarded the winner a $14,250 prize. Today, prize totals reach into the millions.

Several women have raced in various events since NASCAR's beginnings. One of the most influential women in racing history is Janet Guthrie. In May of 1977, Guthrie became the first woman to compete in the famous

Janet Guthrie was the first woman to race in the Indy 500 and Daytona 500.

Indianapolis 500, also known as the Indy 500. She had already raced in the Daytona 500 in February of the same year. In 1978, only one year later, Guthrie again raced at the Indy 500 and crossed the finish line in ninth place. This is a highly respectable placing, and it still remains the best placing by any woman at the Indy 500.

Women in racing are continuing to set records in the twenty-first century. Some of these women include Shawna Robinson and Jennifer Tumminelli of the United States, and Sarah Kavanagh, a 30-year-old racer from Dublin, Ireland. In Great Britain, Penny Mallory became the first woman to drive a World Rally Car in the Network Q Rally of Great Britain.

Not only are there many types of drivers in the world of automobile racing, there are also many varieties of race cars. Single-seater cars, also referred to as Formula One cars, are raced on closed raceways, usually shaped in an oval. Rally race cars are specially constructed production cars that are built to hold up across long distances over different types of terrain that test the endurance of both drivers and vehicles. Stock-car racers drive modified production cars on oval tracks, instead of the single-seaters used in Formula One races. One of the most unusual race cars is the dragster, in which drivers speed down straight tracks to see how fast they can go in a quarter-mile stretch. These cars have long, extended fronts and extra-wide back tires that allow for high speeds and provide the car with enough balance to handle those speeds. Some dragsters can reach the quarter-mile mark in one second at a speed of 330 mph (530 kph). It would take an average automobile nearly 15 seconds to cover the same distance.

Racing's popularity has been aided by other businesses over the past fifty years. Major companies sponsor and promote drivers and races. This affiliation brings Americans who work for those companies and who buy products from those companies into some form of contact with the racing arena.

A stretch dragster has an extra-long front and very wide rear tires that allow it to reach high speeds.

Environmental Pollution

Although racing had a positive cultural influence, it helped contribute to a negative influence of cars on the environment. Exhaust from gas-powered vehicles emits ***carbon monoxide (CO)*** into the atmosphere. Carbon monoxide from cars is created when gasoline isn't completely burned at the combustion point.

Early car engines emitted a lot more CO than today's cleaner-burning engines do. When cars and trucks increased in number over such a short amount of time, the air-pollution problem also increased. Cleaning up the air by making cleaner-running engines wasn't easy. The U.S. government had to pass new laws before exhaust emissions became better controlled.

With nearly 500 million vehicles emitting carbon monoxide, air pollution is at dangerously high levels.

Monitoring Exhaust Emissions

The ***Environmental Protection Agency (EPA)*** is a branch of the U.S. government devoted to protecting the environment.

EPA AND THE CLEAN AIR ACT

The EPA combined a variety of groups that were concerned about protecting the environment. The agency was formed in response to public demonstrations about the poor quality of air and land due to industrial and automobile pollution.

The passage of the EPA's recommendations as the Clean Air Act helped start some of today's pollution controls. Although there is still progress to be made in keeping the environment clean, the laws to protect the land and air might not have passed without the Clean Air Act or the EPA's involvement.

In 1971 the EPA held hearings to determine the amount of harmful emissions that should be allowed to come from gas-powered vehicles. It contacted automobile manufacturers all around the world, asking them to submit their proposals for reducing toxic emissions. Proposals came from more than thirty companies.

By 1975 the EPA put certain regulations into place to reduce harmful emissions. Some of these included the installation of warning buzzers and lights in cars and trucks to alert drivers to possible problems with their exhaust systems. Other regulations had to do with installing and servicing **catalytic converters**, which filter harmful emissions in exhaust systems.

Oil Needs and Oil Problems

The need for huge amounts of gasoline required for all the cars, trucks, buses, and tractors now in use around the world created a great demand for oil, from which gasoline is derived. The biggest oil-producing countries are located in the Middle East and include Saudi Arabia and Iraq. Crude oil, or unprocessed oil, is loaded onto large ships called oil tankers and carried across the oceans to other nation's shores.

A major problem with loading huge quantities of oil onto one ship is that the ship could have a problem while in open waters. **Oil spills** can occur if the ship is wrecked or has a malfunction that ruptures the oil containers. Oil spills have contaminated ocean and shore life around the globe.

The environmental problems caused by automobiles increase with each new car put on the road. Although the awareness of air and oil pollution has increased, so has the world's desire for more automobiles.

Driving Into the Future

Automobile sales totaled $6.7 million in 1950 and $9.3 million in 1965. Eighty-three percent of all those sales took place in the United States. By the late 1950s and early 1960s, Toyota and Datsun had begun production. These automakers, along with Honda, eventually drew interest from Americans. The fuel economy of their cars became more appreciated in the 1970s, as more Americans paid attention to the problems driving caused for the environment and experienced a gasoline shortage.

One remarkable design burst onto the highways in the 1980s. This type of vehicle allowed a better way for large groups of people to travel in comfort. Chrysler came up with what it termed the "minivan" in 1984. This van had two seats up front, two seats in the middle, and a bench-type seat in the rear. The van also had a sliding side door that allowed for easy access. Now large families or youth groups could travel more comfortably, while the driver still had the fuel economy and comfort of a large sedan.

It is clear that the United States is dependent on automobiles and the fuel that powers them. This is reflected in the top businesses of 2002.

A popular type of vehicle to emerge during the 1980s was the minivan.

AUTOMOBILES AND PETROLEUM

The *2002 Scholastic Book of World Records* lists three automobile manufacturers in the list of the world's five largest industrial companies. They are General Motors (number one), Ford Motor Company (number three), and Daimler-Chrysler (number five). Exxon Mobil, USA, which is a *petroleum* company, is number four.

Since the invention of the gas-powered automobile, petroleum, also known as crude oil, has been essential. Without oil that can be made into gasoline, there would be no gas-powered automobile.

With the popularity of the automobile came a greater number of supersized cars and trucks on the world's roads, especially in the United States. This led to a need for more fuel, which often pushed oil and gasoline prices up.

Alternatively Powered Automobiles

Because of the world's dependence on gasoline and oil imports, and because of pollution caused by oil, some automakers looked for different ways to power automobiles. Electric-powered cars were the first alternatively powered vehicles. They are powered completely by batteries, so there is no gas, no spark, and no combustion used to propel the vehicles. A continuous current of electricity is used to power these vehicles. Some advantages of electric cars are that they produce no exhaust, they are quiet, they are simpler to operate because they have fewer parts, and they are easy to maintain. But they also have drawbacks. Most early electric cars required too many batteries to give the car any real power. The batteries didn't stay charged for very long. This meant the electric cars could only travel short distances before needing to be recharged. Another drawback is the smaller size needed to make the vehicles light-weight enough to run on just battery power.

Solar-powered cars were powered by solar panels that recharged batteries, which converted the power into electricity to run the vehicles. They

A woman recharges her electric car in Tokyo, Japan.

had problems similar to those of the basic electric cars, however, which never made them popular with the general public.

The U.S. government wanted to encourage automakers to work harder at producing a powerful, reliable, and practical alternatively powered vehicle. It introduced the **Hybrid-Electric Vehicle (HEV)** Program in 1993. The program was a cost-shared, five-year research partnership among the U.S. Department of Energy, General Motors, Ford Motor Company, and Daimler-Chrysler. This partnership's goal was to develop HEVs. They defined HEVs as vehicles that could use both gasoline and electrical power and would achieve twice the fuel economy of similar vehicles powered only by gas. By 2004 Toyota, Honda, and Ford had offered some type of hybrid vehicle to the public for sale. HEVs combine the internal combustion engine of a gas-powered vehicle with the battery and electric motor of an electric vehicle. These cars use half the fuel to drive the same distance gas-powered vehicles use. Another benefit of HEVs is that they produce many fewer harmful, polluting emissions.

Better fuel economy, less air pollution, and the versatility of the HEV for personal driving and commercial hauling made HEVs a popular innovation in the automobile industry as the twenty-first century began.

Other Innovations

As the automobile celebrated its hundredth birthday in 1993, many changes were made that improved driver comfort and safety. In the early 2000s some car owners could choose to have computer screens on their dashboards. With these touch screens, drivers could start the air conditioner, check fuel economy, or tune the radio to a favorite station.

Some minivans and sport-utility vehicles now have video screens and video players. These multipassenger vehicles also offer rear air-conditioning and drink holders—all designed to enhance passengers' comfort during long trips. **Global Positioning Systems (GPSs)** allow drivers to know exactly where they are if they become lost or have an emergency on the road. The GPS bounces signals from the vehicle to a satellite, which helps drivers monitor their location.

Automobiles changed the world by giving the average person the ability to travel farther than he or she ever could have by foot or by horse. Although the first vehicles were quite a bit different from the cars of today, one thing remains the same: Drivers and passengers love zooming around roads in their cars and trucks.

Global Positioning Systems help a driver navigate with on-board maps and directions.

The Automobile: A Timeline

Karl Benz mounts a gasoline-powered engine onto a tricycle body.
p. 26

Thirteen Duryea cars are built in this year, making them the first production cars.
p. 31

The Red Flag Act becomes the first traffic law.
p. 13

The Duryea brothers design their first car.
p. 30

1769 — 1865 — 1876 — 1886 — 1889 — 1893 — 1895 — 1896

The first machine-propelled, steam-powered road vehicle is built.
p. 12

Nikolaus Otto builds the first four-stroke engine.
p. 25

George Selden is granted a patent for a "self-propelled vehicle powered by internal-combustion engine."
p. 37

Gottlieb Daimler and Wilhem Maybach build a gas-powered, four-wheeled vehicle.
p. 29

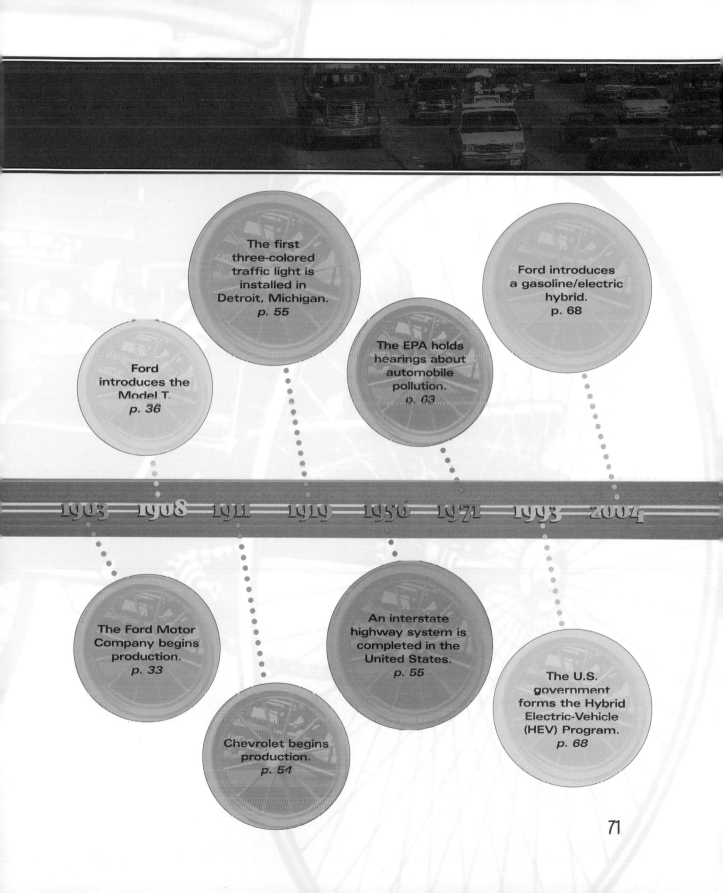

The first three-colored traffic light is installed in Detroit, Michigan.
p. 55

Ford introduces a gasoline/electric hybrid.
p. 68

Ford introduces the Model T.
p. 36

The EPA holds hearings about automobile pollution.
p. 63

1903   1908   1911   1919   1956   1971   1993   2004

The Ford Motor Company begins production.
p. 33

An interstate highway system is completed in the United States.
p. 55

The U.S. government forms the Hybrid Electric-Vehicle (HEV) Program.
p. 68

Chevrolet begins production.
p. 54

71

Glossary

brake system: the pads and fluid lines that create friction on a car's wheels to slow and stop the vehicle

carbon monoxide (CO): an odorless gas produced from burning carbon or from an incomplete combustion of gasoline

catalytic converter: a part attached to the exhaust system that reduces harmful emissions

chassis: the frame and body of a vehicle

crankshaft: a long, tubular shaft that rotates when the pistons move downward and moves gears in the transmission

differential: gearboxes on the axles that allow steering

electric starter: an electrical device that directs a current from the battery to start the engine

Environmental Protection Agency (EPA): a branch of government dedicated to protecting the land, air, and water from all types of pollution

four-stroke, gas-powered engine: an internal-combustion, gas-powered engine that uses a four-step process of intake, compression, explosion, and exhaust to create power

Global Positioning System (GPS): a device that emits a signal to a satellite, which verifies the specific location of that device

Hybrid-Electric Vehicle (HEV): a vehicle that combines the internal-combustion engine and the electric motor of an electric vehicle

ignition system: components that control the igniting of fuel in the engine's cylinders to start a motor

magnetos: electric generators that direct a magnetic current

oil spills: leakages of petroleum from an oil tanker or other vehicle

petroleum: a thick, dark, oily liquid found deep underground that, in its raw form, can be used as a fuel or be separated (by distilling) into gasoline

piston chamber: housing in the engine that contains the pistons

quadracyle: Henry Ford's self-propelled, gas-powered, four-wheeled vehicle

spark plug: the device inside the cylinder with two points that allow an electric spark to pass through and ignite the gas

transmission: system of gears that regulate power from the crankshaft to vary the speed of a vehicle

two-stroke engine: internal-combustion engine that allows a continuous flow of fuel and oil mix into the piston chamber

To Find Out More

Books

Lord, Trevor. *Big Book of Cars*. New York: Dorling Kindersley Publishing, 1999.

Sutton, Richard. *Car* (Eyewitness Books). New York: Alfred A. Knopf, 1990.

Wilson, Anthony. *Visual Timeline of Transportation*. New York: Dorling Kindersley Publishing, 1995.

Web Sites

Henry Ford Museum

www.hfmgv.org

This site lists many of Henry Ford's historical accomplishments, provides his biography, and lists Ford Motor Company news items.

Indianapolis Motor Speedway

www.brickyard.com

This site contains everything anyone could ever want to know about the famous Indy 500 race.

Professional Auto Racing

www.factmonster.com/ipka.A0771589.html

This is an excellent, student-friendly source all about professional race-car driving.

Organizations

The Alliance of Automobile Manufacturers

1401 Eye Street, N.W., Suite 900

Washington, DC 20005

Antique Automobile Club of America

501 W. Governor Road

P.O. Box 417

Hershey, PA 17033

Index

About the Author

Learning to drive is the dream of most teenagers. Researching and writing this book helped author Robyn Conley remember the freedom that her first car gave her. While cruising through race-car sites and books about engines, she tried to keep the thrill of driving in mind.

Much of the research for this book was made possible by the invention of the automobile. Automobiles allowed the author to take trips to the library to study books about engines, Henry Ford, race-car driving, and the history of the automobile. Other sources helped, too, such as the Web sites listed in this book and many others.

Conley enjoys writing and speaking about writing. When she's not busy at her desk, she often substitute teaches middle-grade students in the small community of Clyde in West Texas. For Franklin Watts, Conley has written *Motion Pictures* in the Inventions That Shaped the World series.